I LIKE **REPTILES** AND **AMPHIBIANS!**

FUN FACTS ABOUT
ALLIGATORS!

Carmen Bredeson

Enslow Elementary

an imprint of

Enslow Publishers, Inc.

40 Industrial Road
Box 398
Berkeley Heights, NJ 07922
USA

http://www.enslow.com

CONTENTS

WORDS TO KNOW 3

PARTS OF AN ALLIGATOR 3

WHERE DO ALLIGATORS LIVE? 4

HOW ARE ALLIGATORS AND
CROCODILES DIFFERENT? 6

HOW DO ALLIGATORS SWIM? 9

WHAT DO ALLIGATORS EAT? 10

HOW DO ALLIGATORS CATCH
THEIR FOOD? 13

DO ALLIGATORS CHEW
THEIR FOOD? 14

HOW BIG DO ALLIGATORS
GROW? 17

WHERE DO ALLIGATORS
LAY EGGS? 19

WHAT IS THE LIFE CYCLE OF
AN ALLIGATOR? 20

LEARN MORE
  BOOKS 22   WEB SITES 23

INDEX 24

WORDS TO KNOW

crocodile (KRAH kuh dyl)—A kind of reptile that looks like an alligator.

lunge (LUHNJ)—To move forward suddenly.

prey (PRAY)—An animal that is food for another animal.

webbed (WEBD)—Having skin between fingers or toes.

PARTS OF AN ALLIGATOR

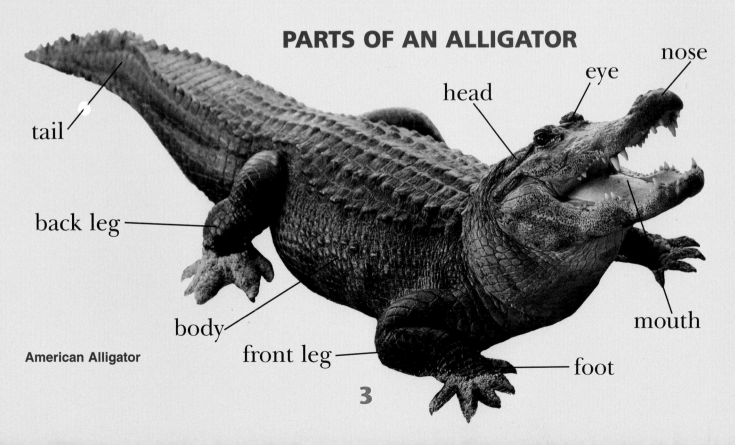

nose

eye

head

tail

back leg

body

front leg

mouth

foot

American Alligator

3

WHERE DO ALLIGATORS LIVE?

Alligators like wet, warm places. They live in swamps, lakes, ponds, and rivers. Most alligators live in South America. In North America, they live near the Gulf of Mexico.

American Alligators live in the red area of the map.

HOW ARE ALLIGATORS AND CROCODILES DIFFERENT?

American Alligator

An alligator's top jaw is shaped like the letter U. A **crocodile**'s is shaped like the letter V. When a crocodile closes its mouth, you can still see long, sharp teeth.

Crocodile

Alligators can swim very fast!

HOW DO ALLIGATORS SWIM?

An alligator's tail is very strong. It moves back and forth in the water. *Swish*. *Swish*. Its feet are **webbed** like duck feet. They help steer, or move, the alligator through the water.

An alligator's left front foot

webbing

9

WHAT DO ALLIGATORS EAT?

Little alligators eat insects, small fish, and shrimp. Bigger alligators eat turtles, snakes, and birds.

Great big alligators need more food. They may eat deer, wild pigs, and small cows.

This alligator catches a bird with its powerful jaws.

10

HOW DO
ALLIGATORS
CATCH THEIR FOOD?

Alligators spend most of their time in water. They swim very quietly. Only the alligator's nose and eyes are above the water. The alligator spots a meal! It **lunges** out of the water with its mouth open and grabs it.

DO
ALLIGATORS
CHEW THEIR FOOD?

When an alligator attacks, its jaws close down HARD! The alligator may drag its **prey** under the water to drown it. Then it tears the animal apart and swallows the pieces whole. An alligator does not chew its food.

Alligators can run very fast on land.
This alligator has caught a tasty turtle!

An alligator's tail is about as long as the rest of its body.

HOW BIG DO ALLIGATORS GROW?

Alligators keep growing their whole lives. The longer they live, the bigger they get. Most alligators grow to be about ten feet long. The biggest alligator ever found was more than nineteen feet long!

WHERE DO
ALLIGATORS
LAY EGGS?

A mother alligator scoops up a big pile of dirt and sticks. She digs a hole in the middle of the pile and lays up to fifty eggs. Then she covers up the hole with more dirt. She stays close to guard her nest.

WHAT IS THE
LIFE CYCLE
OF AN
ALLIGATOR?

1. Mother alligator builds a nest and lays her eggs.

2. The eggs hatch in about nine weeks. Mother alligator digs her babies out of the nest.

3. She scoops them into her mouth and carries them to the water. She teaches them to swim and find food. After about ten years, they can have babies too.

These baby alligators are going for a ride!

LEARN MORE

BOOKS

Clarke, Ginjer. *Baby Alligator*. New York: Grosset & Dunlap, 2000.

Jefferis, David, and Tony Allen. *Alligator*. Austin, Tex.: Raintree Steck-Vaughn, 2001.

McCarthy, Colin. *Reptile*. New York: Dorling Kindersley Publishing, 2000.

American Alligator

WEB SITES

Enchanted Learning

<http://www.enchantedlearning.com/subjects/reptiles/alligator/
Alligator.shtml>

San Diego Zoo

<http://www.sandiegozoo.org/animalbytes/t-crocodile.html>

American Alligator

INDEX

American Alligator

Babies 21
biggest 17
Crocodile 6
Eggs 19, 20–21

Feet 9

Jaw 6, 14

Nest 19, 20–21

Prey 10, 14

Tail 9, 16
teeth 6

A Note About Reptiles and Amphibians:

Amphibians can live on land or in water. Frogs, toads, and salamanders are amphibians.
Reptiles have skin covered with scales. Snakes, alligators, turtles, and lizards are reptiles.

Enslow Elementary, an imprint of Enslow Publishers, Inc.

Enslow Elementary® is a registered trademark of Enslow Publishers, Inc.

Library of Congress Cataloging-in-Publication Data

Bredeson, Carmen.
    Fun facts about alligators! / Carmen Bredeson.
        p. cm. — (I like reptiles and amphibians!)
    Includes bibliographical references (p.   ) and index.
    ISBN-13: 978-0-7660-2786-2
    ISBN-10: 0-7660-2786-4
    1. Alligators—Juvenile literature. I. Title.
    QL666.C925B74 2007
    597.98'4—dc22

                                    2006024347

Printed in the United States of America

10 9 8 7 6 5 4 3 2 1

Every effort has been made to locate all copyright holders of material used in this
book. If any errors or omissions have occurred, corrections will be made in future
editions of this book.

Photo Credits: Andre Jenny / Painet Inc., p. 16; Artville, p. 5 (map); © C.C.
Lockwood 2007, pp. 18, 20, 21; © C.C. Lockwood / Animals Animals, p. 11; Connie
Bransilver/Photo Researchers, Inc., p, 13; © Francois Gohier / Ardea.com, pp. 4–5;
Getty Images / Michele Westmorland, p. 15; Getty Images / Stephen Cooper, p. 8;
© 2006 Jupiterimages Corporation, pp. 1, 10, 22; © Masa Ushioda / Visuals
Unlimited, p. 12; Photo courtesy http://www.philip.greenspun.com, p. 6;
Shutterstock, pp. 2, 7, 23; Warren Photographic, p. 3; Wing-Chi Poon, Wikipedia.org,
p. 9.

Cover Photograph: © Zigmund Leszczynski / Animals Animals

Series Science Consultant:
Raoul Bain
Herpetology Biodiversity Specialist
Center for Biodiversity and
    Conservation
American Museum of Natural History
New York, NY

Series Literacy Consultant:
Allan A. De Fina, Ph.D.
Past President of the New Jersey
    Reading Association
Professor, Department of Literacy Education
New Jersey City University
Jersey City, NJ